A GIFT

OTHER BOOKS BY DAVID R. SLAVITT

POETRY
Big Nose
The Carnivore
Child's Play
Day Sailing
Dozens
The Eclogues and the Georgics of Virgil
Eight Longer Poems
The Elegies to Delia of Albius Tibullus
Equinox
The Fables of Avianus
Five Plays of Seneca
The Metamorphoses of Ovid
Ovid's Poetry of Exile
Rounding the Horn
Suits for the Dead
Vital Signs: New and Selected Poems
The Walls of Thebes

FICTION
ABCD
The Agent (with Bill Adler)
Alice at 80
Anagrams
The Cliff
Cold Comfort
Feel Free
The Hussar
Jo Stern
The Killing of the King
King of Hearts
Lives of the Saints
The Outer Mongolian
Ringer
Rochelle; or, Virtue Rewarded
Salazar Blinks
Short Stories Are Not Real Life
Turkish Delights

NONFICTION
Physicians Observed
Understanding Social Psychology (with Paul Secord and Carl Backman)
Virgil

EDITED COLLECTIONS
The Johns Hopkins Complete Roman Drama (with Palmer Bovie)
Land of Superior Mirages: New and Selected Poems of Adrien Stoutenberg

A Gift

The Life of da Ponte

A Poem by David R. Slavitt

Louisiana State University Press
Baton Rouge and London
1996

Manufactured in the United States of America
First printing
05 04 03 02 01 00 99 98 97 96 5 4 3 2 1

Designer: Melanie O'Quinn Samaha
Typeface: Janson Text
Printer and binder: Thomson-Shore, Inc.

LIBRARY OF CONGRESS CATALOGING-IN-PUBLICATION DATA

Slavitt, David R., date.
A gift : the life of da Ponte : a poem / by David R. Slavitt.
p. cm.
ISBN 0-8071-2047-2 (alk. paper). —ISBN 0-8071-2048-0 (pbk. : alk. paper)
1. Da Ponte, Lorenzo, 1749–1838—Poetry. 2. Librettists—Italy—Poetry. 3. Italian Americans—Poetry. I. Title.
PS3569.L3G54 1996
811'.54—dc20 95-39360
CIP

A portion of this poem appeared previously, in slightly different form, in *Chronicles*, and another portion appears in *Classical, Renaissance, and Postmodernist Acts of the Imagination: Essays Commemorating O. B. Hardison, Jr.*, edited by Arthur F. Kinney (University of Delaware Press, 1996).

The paper in this book meets the guidelines for permanence and durability of the Committee on Production Guidelines for Book Longevity of the Council on Library Resources. ∞

For Mac and Auntie Ruth

A GIFT

To be picked up and then
put down, discarded,
not only by Amadeus (bad enough)
but by the gods themselves . . .

If New York was real, the grocery store and the job
at Columbia College (teaching Italian), then Mozart
was a dream and their collaboration a dream.
Or, if that was real, then this was all nightmare
from which he might yet rouse to break the surface
like some great sea beast, streaming tears of terror
and gratitude.

In Ceneda, Emanuele was born to Geremia
and Rachele Conegliano, after whose death

Geremia courted a Christian woman—
girl, really—Orasala Pasqua Paietta.
The laws required conversion before the wedding,
the children's too. They took the name of the local
bishop, da Ponte. The father became at a stroke
Gasparo, and his eldest son, Lorenzo.
And Emanuele?

Disappears.

No mention of those first fourteen years;
they slip from his memoirs if not his mind,
with the other, earlier name, the other religion.

A matter of small steps, from the catechism
to further, subtler questions—what a bright lad
deserves and can only get by taking orders,
minor ones first, to go to the seminary,
and then, when the bishop dies

and his father suffers

reverses, priestly vows
so he can continue study at Portogruaro.

He did believe

(as much as any Borgia)

in the Church

as theater.

Transport, flight, and then a precipitous fall,
in art as in life.
With women, for instance, in Venice,
those libertine years.
He and Casanova knew each other,
and disapproved of each other.
Angiola
Tiepolo was the first, gorgeous, hot tempered—
her elder brother, Girolamo, was bad,
a gambler, almost Angiola's pimp
(some suspected worse).
They were not part of the plan.

To have a plan, however vague,
the sense of a career,
a talent coming into its own, was the least
a clever fellow like that would owe himself.

To float, drift, see again and again
the sun dip down and waters of the lagoon

turn black as velvet glinting with torch-light brilliants
was to reckon in self-loathing the cost of every
moment of pleasure:
                                        the sin was the waste of time.

From Venice then in flight,
before the arrest warrant of the Council of Ten
could impede him, to safety, across the border—
into Gorizia, and the arms of an innkeeper there,
a gorgeous woman,
                                    German, or maybe Slovenian.
He never knew,
spoke neither language, and she had no Italian.
But they made clear enough their instant lust.

The best days of his life, that long wallow,
                                                        a paradise.
At length, his money ran out.
She left a purse of gold coins under the pillow,
which he, in pride, refused.

The idyll was over
in any event, a dream more vivid than most

but lacking the disagreeable, credible grit
of impatience or mere inattention.
                                        Love is not
that simple initial soaring.

Those amazing days betrayed—
and were betrayed by—the rest of his life.

Joseph II, now that Maria Theresa,
his mum, was dead, was Emperor and could do
whatever he liked. He chose to be liberal, nice,
and dress like a modest burgher.
(He warned his sister Marie Antoinette
that her showy extravagance was dangerous.)

Waving his hand in the air,
he decreed he no longer liked Singspiel.
Genug!
Let there be Italians again.

Da Ponte arrived at the right moment, parlayed
introductions to reach at last the
        GRAND CHAMBERLAIN'S OFFICE

where, talking fast, he got himself appointed
Burgtheater Poet.
                    Confirmed, in course, by Joseph,
before whom da Ponte came.

                              "How many
plays have you written, signore?" His Majesty asks.
"None, sire." (This, in terror.)

                              The Emperor
smiles and jokes: "Splendid. A virgin muse."

The virgin learned soon enough the whorey tricks:
Adaptation, translation, theft,
                         the politics
of opera houses—managers with their passions
for special effects (bells and birds were in fashion),
the prima donnas jealous of one another,
the soprano ingenue (not to mention her mother),
and the composer, a collaborator but
at any moment he'll turn on you and cut
the best lines in the whole book, or reverse
their order, and change the meter.
                              Your empty purse
won't let you argue back. A *suggeritore*,

it prompts you to agree at once. The story,
a dismal one, was familiar enough to go
with a graceful minor-key continuo.

Hack work corrodes the spirit, grinds you down,
destroys your self-respect. Destroys you.
Il ricco d'un giorno (from Bertati's text)
was the dumbest of the three ideas he'd offered:
of course Salieri picked it.

The mad hope
                    grows like a mold on bread
that it's not so bad,
                         is better than you think—
but what that means
is only that your judgment is going too,
you can't tell good from bad, are a fraud, impostor,
and sooner or later will be exposed. Why not
quit now?
          Get out
                    with some dignity left . . .
And go where?

So you dip your quill again
into the poisoned inkwell, scrawl more words,
and hope that in the general disaster
no one will notice which shortcomings were yours.

A catastrophe: shuffling feet and laughter,
catcalls even. Salieri's music was wretched
("stolen from everywhere!"—so Zinzendorf),
and the singing none too good. No one excused
the libretto either.

They did it again, and again,
six times in all, each performance a torture
for everyone.

Salieri walked away
swearing never to work with da Ponte again.
The Emperor, nevertheless, demanded another,
if only to keep the appointment from going to Casti,
whom Casanova called "buffoon and pimp."
(The Emperor didn't like Casanova either.)
"You must pluck up your courage again," he told da Ponte,
"and give us another."

A blessing, was it, or curse?

Meanwhile, the teeth, the pain of teeth, the griefs
of dentistry . . . A love triangle also,
with a girl who loved da Ponte, while another,
Doriguti, a fellow lodger, fellow
Italian, loved the girl.

                                        And in his pain,
da Ponte, with an abscess, was willing to try
the cure Doriguti offered—engraver's acid,
which nearly killed him.

                                        All his teeth fell out.
For two years he could hardly keep down the little
he'd managed to gum and, without gagging, swallow
in pain,
humiliation,
wretchedness.

But then a change in fortune—nothing to bank on,
except that misfortune is not reliable either.
If we assume intention somewhere, the relenting
may only be to keep our hopes alive
that they may torment us further, as torturers do,

who learn how far they can go and still bring back
from oblivion's lip their broken quivering subjects.

That, too, is misleading:
there's no plan to it,
no sense.

Martín y Soler,
just arrived in Vienna, needed a book.
Protégé of the Spanish ambassador's wife,
he got himself introduced to Emperor Joseph,
who passed him on to da Ponte with prompt result:
The Good-Hearted Grouch.
                    It was Goldoni's play
cut down, done up, reworked.
                    He was luckier now,
or maybe he'd picked up the knack from reading,
going to hear performances, paying attention:
reduction and embellishment,
reshaping prose into singable verse . . .
A witchy business,
you never know, until the composer sets it,
how well or badly you've done.
                    (You still can't say
for sure, knowing he could have taken good
work and words and wrecked them, ruined them all.)

But rousing applause
from start to finish—even for recitatives.
A success, or at least enough so that offers of work
came in from several composers, including one
who'd enjoyed, four years before, a degree of success
with a piece in German on Turkish harems—
Mozzart
(which is how da Ponte spelled it all his life).

A genius, but they all claim that.
                                                            A boor,
as if to defy the world to recognize
beneath the boorishness his real refinement.
And a fondness for crude jokes.

What can one say of such a passage?
Da Ponte claimed and believed
his poetry was the door through which that music came,
the emotions and wit of his librettos
gave rise to those of the music.

But look at that last
Masonic nonsense, incoherent, almost

insane . . .

Die Zauberflöte.

As if to deny da Ponte any credit.

The start was awkward
and their first meeting inauspicious.
Mozart explained his distaste (one tried to smile)
for rhymes
as well as his fondness for farce,
even slapstick.
Da Ponte put the best face on it he could,
needing the work.
He gets no credit for that.

He was, as if on a child's whim, first picked up
and then dropped,
ignored, and left to disappear
beneath a chair
servants ought to be cleaning under but don't.

Their theme, at first and all along: forgiveness,
a relenting that da Ponte had all but despaired of and yet
had sometimes imagined coming down from heaven,

an angel's gift—
                                        the angel looked like his mother,
or else that woman he'd known at the inn,
or some conflation, confection of all the others
who'd shown him teasing glimpses
of what the world
                                        ought to have been.

Tormented as we are,
we suppose we have deserved it—and therefore pray
as Almaviva does at the end,
"Perdono!"
kneeling down before the contessa,
"Perdono!"

With Mozart, that odd, coarse, brilliant fellow,
he found, at least for a while,
the relenting of which he'd dreamed.

At the time, it was nothing, another job of work,
another composer to please. It seemed to go well,
but they never had the success da Ponte expected.

But did they know how good they were? Did they realize,
themselves, and could they believe in what they felt,
at least sometimes?

Da Ponte was never sure what Mozart thought.

For himself . . . ?

Not really.

No.

Rhymes, at times like chimes: their ringing
into his head was a way of bringing
the balance of honor back toward level.
Let Mozart hate them and go to the devil.
Ed in vece del fandango
Una marcia per il fango,
Per montagne, per valloni,
Colle nevi e i sollioni,
Al concerto de trombone . . .

Da Ponte held his ground, let him chew on that,
and Mozart did; and out of Figaro's mouth
came music one would die to hear in heaven.

And then, in Prague,
Domenico Guardasoni, the impresario there, made them a decent
offer: they had a success with Bertati's libretto
for Gazzaniga's opera, *réchauffé.*

What da Ponte remembers: how they all behaved
as if he'd written their parts, scribbling fast
and laughing to himself.

At the Duscheks' house,
Casanova is there (now reduced
to librarian and pet of Count Waldstein),
the singers, of course,
                                        and Mozart,
who says he is going to town, horrifying them all.
The overture, he has sworn, is in his head,
but musicians are not psychics,
                                                      require a score,
all the parts copied out.
                                                They contrive therefore
a plot:
            Signora Bondini asks the composer
to fetch the gloves she has left on the harpsichord.

When Mozart goes in to get them, they lock him in
and tell him he can't leave
until he's produced
the music.

He asks for candles, paper, pens,
cakes, and wine, and these the company brings him,
hoisting them up to the windowsill with poles
from the grape arbor.
Da Ponte passes up
a pot,
and the maestro, laughing, calls down not
his thanks but regrets that he can't fill it
and pour it
down
on da Ponte's
despicable
head.
Laughter. Blackout.
A grand success
for the opening then in Prague of *Il dissoluto*
punito; o sia, Il don Giovanni.
Da Ponte,
called back to Vienna,
misses his moment.

As if he were Masetto, and God the Don
who's decided he is a churl and doesn't deserve
even a brief taste of such a sweetness.

In Vienna, however, a consolation: the singer,
La Ferrarese, or Adriana Gabrieli.
Nancy Storace had gone away to London,
and singing her roles
                                        was this one,
with a huge range from alto to coloratura.
Stocky, really, and not an accomplished actress,
but with fire there in the eyes,
the heart,
                the voice,
                                    she struck
fire in a listener.
In him.

They set up another complicated business—
he, La Ferrarese, and her husband,
one del Bene, with whom, for a change, da Ponte
was on good terms.

And where are the rules for these things set down,
how should men behave? Or women?

At the theater, trouble,
their patron, the Emperor, worried about the costs
of his entertainments. Also—some said—ailing,
but at any rate less smitten by Celestina
Coltellini, the soprano,
                                        his mistress,
whose tiresome tirades he could avoid
by shutting down the theater.

They could all go away and leave him in peace . . .

Da Ponte begged permission to carry on,
to find the money somehow, from the Viennese
bon ton.
                    Weary, Joseph scribbled his name
to the piece of paper.

With all this, *Così fan tutte*, to show
how funny it is, precarious, grotesque,
and yet one can contrive to behave with style,
as the women do at the end, in their curious triumph
where it's never clear which one winds up with Guglielmo

and which with Ferrando.
Still, the music plays,
cheerily, heartily, heartlessly on.

Mozart and he had hoped to share those zecchini
the gentlemen on stage so prized,
but five performances only . . .
                                        Then the theater
closed
for the Emperor's death.

His brother, Leopold, came from Tuscany
to take in hand the affairs of a somewhat disordered
state.
        Everywhere, spies,
                              informers,
                                        agents provocateurs.

Even the theater,
                    especially there.

The Ferrarese's contract was running out.
Da Ponte could tell how the wind was blowing.
                                                  Letters,
frantic letters—to St. Petersburg,

where his friend Martín y Soler might work him
an appointment
                    as court poet of Russia . . . ?
Or maybe London,
where he and Mozart might find some job together?
(Mozart had that bizarre Masonic pageant
and couldn't think of leaving—not for months.)

Under that pressure, the truth comes out,
his belief that he is a fraud
                              will be found out,
impostor, apostate,
mountebank . . .

His plots
depended always on such devices
with actors changing their costumes
and acting at one remove,
acting at acting:
Susanna and Rosina in Almaviva's garden,
or the Don and Leporello
under Elvira's window—
for the thrill of it,

the desperation of it,
or merely the knowledge that whatever it is
cannot long continue:
mortality but concentrated,
life.

Then in *Così* that insane Albanian business.
In grotesque getups the callow fellows
find true selves and true loves . . .

And then lose them?
It is not clear.

Da Ponte is waiting to see
what will happen, hoping, and yet too shrewd
to suppose it can go on much longer.

Like a mother,
a run of good luck will sicken, die,
and leave you
orphaned,
renamed,
unselfed,
undone.

A sordid business, enemies everywhere.
Later they seemed almost benign,
indifferent tools of a hostile fate.
Had it not been they, there would have been others,
supernumerary villains,
                                        a chorus of envy,
spite, and betrayal.
In opera companies, these are not hard to find,
or anywhere else.

Consider Piticchio, Sgrilli,
Lattanzi, Bussani, Thorwart, and Salieri,
limp face cards of the deck
with which Leopold played games of patience
Da Ponte lost,
        out of favor,
                        office,
                                        and Vienna.

A guttering then, or the slow fading-away
of hope, intention, direction . . .

He tried Trieste
and, living from hand to mouth,
he took the hand of Nancy, an English girl—
properly Ann Celestine Ernestine Grahl,
a trader's daughter.
A dalliance, at first, and then . . .

She had assumed he would marry her.
He tried to hide his surprise
that any woman would want him for a husband.

He hadn't the heart to refuse her so poor a reward
if that was what she wanted.

He was selling his clothing to buy food.
He had heard the dismal news
that Mozart was dead.

Mozzart dead?
Why not then? Or why?
Numb, stricken, he married her.
Ordained, a priest,
he may have performed the ceremony himself,
but they were somehow, anyhow, joined
and set out together for Paris,

where Marie Antoinette might open her purse or arrange
employment of some kind for him.

In August of 1792?

Who would have guessed
the tumbrel, already built,
waited to carry her off?
On the road, they made a stop
at Oberleutensdorf, to visit amico
Giacomo,
               but Casanova was broke,
                                        was penniless:
da Ponte would not embarrass
himself or his acquaintance by asking for help.

To Dresden, then, to see Mazzolà,
whose welcome was cautious at best,
not needing, in that small town,
any rival poet.

So off to Paris,
but the queen was imprisoned.
                                   They heard the news at the border
and headed instead for London,

where Nancy's sister and brother-in-law were living,
getting by but just barely.
                                        No help at all from them.

Bread for breakfast, da Ponte remembered, bread
for lunch,
and supper only salty tears.
To Casanova's suggestion he teach Italian,
da Ponte wrote back, "It is a low profession
followed by waiters, cobblers, exiles, cops . . .
who have by way of payment only
                                                    coppers."

A commission, then, for a new libretto, from diva
Gertrud Mara providing thirty guineas . . .
But it never happened.
Meanwhile he watched his pile
dwindle down as he kept up his appearance
buying clothes to impress,
                                        or at least not distress,
the Duke of Bedford,
the Marquis of Salisbury.
All their polite interest came to nothing.

Casanova wrote to cheer him,
observing that he was not without assets,
Nancy's, for instance.
                                        Da Ponte replied in anger,
he would rather die than pimp his wife that way
to some milord.

Like a guttering candle, he shot bright bursts
of impotent anger into a gloom
that toyed with him.
Was it God's punishment?
Or only a proof that his unbelief was right?

Again, he was selling clothing to buy food.

To Belgium, then, to try his prospects there,
start an opera company . . .
Nothing, nothing.
Only the costs of the journey.
Then a letter
that William Taylor, in London, "Opera Taylor"
manager and part owner of Kings Theatre,
wanted him, even needed him.

A reprieve!
A life preserver thrown to a drowning man
from the deck of a sinking ship.
Taylor's debts were grand,
his dreams impossible,
his troupe a continuing wrangle,
his audiences loutish,
or at least impatient—
it was da Ponte's job
to cut down, speed up, tighten,
and not bore the London boors.

They wouldn't do Mozart
whose music was not "fit for the English taste."

Still, it was recognizable, a version
of what he had known in Vienna,
                                        a ground for hope
that something good might happen,
some combination
of opportunity, inspiration, and luck . . .
Not another Mozart, perhaps, but someone
by and with whom he could soar again
to giddiest heights.

Taylor was more or less crazy,
a debtor, living within the King's Bench rules,
and then, by one of those British fancies,
a member of Parliament—
immune from arrest for debt.
Which meant da Ponte, who'd cosigned notes
became the creditors' target,
to whom they could look
for satisfaction.

What kind of world was this?
At what point does bad luck become something more,
a malign fate, visitation, curse?

He is forty-four years old,
and without the teeth looks older.
His hopes for a change
have faded

or, say, corroded,
mock him now.
He knows what he can do—or has done
and might, still, be able to do again
with the right composer,
the right stars.
And no one cares. They have their own lives to lead.

A great thought, a vast vision, but then . . .
                                        gone.
You know you knew for a moment something
wonderful.
                You have learned that thoughts can come back
and whatever triggered this may trigger again
its like, or even its better.
                                You wait, as if
you had some choice.
                            A profound, elating idea,
a lamp about to be relit, a vista,
loved and lost, restored . . .
It will surely happen. It doesn't
happen.
It keeps on
not happening,

and turns into a fiction,
a cruel joke of which you are the butt.

He walks the London streets, another body
in the crowd's jostle and swarm,

his sense of himself, his gift and worth,
a vain pretension.
Each golden morning gives way,
and sooner than the last,
to a dank day and cold, unpleasant night.

And then, from St. Petersburg, his friend,
Martín y Soler, arrived in London!
Together they would turn the world around,
set the clocks back to a better year.

One could make some sense of the Paris terror,
the baskets of heads of aristocrats
a payment for generations of excess,
the fall that pride
is supposed to encounter at last.
He has given thought to his own plight
as a punishment, but his moment of grandeur
was brief—
brief enough
for indulgent gods to have overlooked it.

No good to brood.
And now there was paying work: *The School for Husbands,*
silly, perhaps, but fun (not too demanding

for these inattentive *inglesi*).
It went well enough,
but his friend was changed, had turned.
In the bitter Russian winters, his soul had frozen
hard and dead.
They did another piece, *The Island of Pleasure*,
the composer working and living with da Ponte.
He knocked up one of the servants,
then denied it,
blamed Da Ponte.
They worked on the second act
in silent loathing, imagining, on their island
of ice, an *isola del piacere*.

Mozart, dead,
he missed;
this one, alive,
he wished
dead.
Soler returned at last to Russia.

Da Ponte, himself, dead?
He sometimes thought how an end to the pain
was available,

beckoned beneath the bridges over the Thames
in the cold, black water.

Slowly downward, nevertheless,
into the business of mere business,
the countersigning of bills of exchange, notes, endorsements . . .
He was paid a stipend of sorts,
                                        but never enough.
He devised schemes, only slightly less fanciful
than those his composers set to music.
Libretti, for instance, had to be printed.
Why not keep those profits?
He became an *homme d'affaires*, or at least pretended.
He set up a printing shop.
And Nancy and her sister Louisa he put in business,
a coffeehouse where everyone came,
nobility, gentry, and public at large, to gossip
and discuss, when the curtain came down,
what had gone on,
and how good, or how bad, each one had been.

Then—it's 1798—the soprano
goes off to the continent with her lover,
the baritone.
                    Taylor sends da Ponte
to find replacements, gives him a hundred guineas
and sends him home
                              to Italy again.

The spirit remembers what plants know, the roots'
ramification down in the dirt, its tang
not quite the same anywhere else in the world.
To go back, then, to what you recognize
as your own air, where the taste of water is right . . .

It was Ovid's dream, those years away in Asia,
not merely to go home but to undo
the pain, the mess of promise betrayed. The world
has gone awry and it must be put right.
A child's dream, but who is to say that child
is wrong?

Across the water, then,

and south

to the Veneto, his skin aprickle,
as if he were on his way to an assignation
with one he had loved and believed was lost:
his youth, a truer, better self not yet
betrayed, none of its promises broken.

Winter vines embrace skeleton sticks,
and trees wave their bare branches in welcome.
His eyes, at an empty turn in the road, tear
in joy, regret, chagrin, delight . . .

He rubs

wet sockets with the clumsy fists
of the boy he is no longer,

but can again remember.

In the carriage beside him, his wife stares at the stranger
he has become, wary of what may happen,
and fearful of how he may bear new disappointment.

They part at Castelfranco.
He will go on alone to Ceneda—

his vague but terrible dreads
at war with hopes more vague.

His coach goes on
into familiar country, reaching at last
home ground,
the ambit of his boyhood's walking.

                                        Alighting
some distance from the house, he crosses the square
silently, on foot, so as not to alert them,
stands at his own door and listens to voices,
as we suppose—or once did—angels might,

and when he can no longer bear it, knocks.

"Who's there?"
He disguises his voice, and calls out, "Open!"
and his sister cries, "Lorenzo!"

Then such hugs,
caresses, and tears he thinks he will suffocate.
They take him inside to see his father, Gasparo,
who cannot speak, cannot even move.
                                        They stare,

as parent and child must, reunited in heaven,
their wounds healed,
                    hearts made whole again.

His stepmother is dead eight years,
his brother Girolamo dead,
and brother Luigi.
                    Their father is still in mourning.
His half-sister, Faustina,
now nineteen, he meets for the first time.
Life goes on—a crude saying and cruel,
but true enough.

He stays two nights,
then, lest the charm of the dream wear through
to the nerves' more realistic testimony,
leaves.

To Venice, his other home: he can go there,
the term of his exile having now run out,
and the government changed.

Napoleon's army has come
and, with the Peace of Campoformio, gone.
The Austrians run things now.
Da Ponte approaches
the Piazza San Marco from the land side,
turns a corner to let it suddenly open,
                                        blossom
as it has in his mind,
a treasure,
a known vista
of elegance, grace, civility . . .
                                Desolate,
                                        empty,
only loutish Austrian soldiers everywhere,
its coffeehouses empty, and spies spying
on spies.
It is a comedy.
                It is a wake.

And yet, there is a comfort in it, Venice
conforming this way to what he has gone through,
a coming-down from a vision of grandeur,
the more persuasive because it is gone
and now an indictment.
This city is shabby, mean,

                                        poor, and poor in spirit;
the world is impoverished.
He sickens to see it, but takes the bitter
satisfaction a stricken man might take
to see his neighbors' corpses
carried out for the burial cart.

An old enemy invents some story,
turns him in to the police:
                                          he has to flee
again.
This is his homecoming, this
his nature.

He cannot return to Ceneda.
Padua then, to rendezvous with Nancy,
and on to Bologna and Florence.

He will never see his father again.

Now news from London that old rivals
in the company have combined, patched up their quarrels,
turned on him,

squeezed him out.

A disaster.

He hires a couple of singers
and hurries home.

A cold, difficult journey:
they cross the frozen Elbe,
see the wreck of a coach that didn't make it,
passengers, coachmen, horses all drowned there.
Hamburg harbor is frozen.
Inns are full and expensive.
They stay a month
and then, when the ice breaks up,

at last sail

to a chilly reception from Taylor,
and frigid failure for the singers he hired.

Turned out, then, he turns
to the business of printing libretti and other works
of Italian letters,

and might make a living

but for his friends, his old connections, whose debts
he has endorsed, cosigned, and guaranteed.
Bankruptcy, then, and arrest, again and again,
thirty times in a three-month span.

The small sums that remain are nibbled away
with court costs, lawyers' fees, constables' charges,
carriages, messengers . . .

All the time, he is thinking of what he has done,
what he once achieved, those old grandeurs . . .
They can never take that away, can they?

Nancy has some coffeeshop money put by.
To save that, they decide she should flee
somewhere safe, beyond the reach of clutching
usurers, creditors, bailiffs, their tangle of paper.

Start fresh—at first, it's an idle dream,
then a desperate possibility, then
a plausible idea.
                        She, at least, can go,
to America,
                  where desperate people go,
making the leap to otherness and elsewhere.
She leaves Gravesend in August, 1804,
bound for Philadelphia.

He puts her on Captain Collet's vessel, hugs her,
turns away, and only then

understands that death cannot be worse,
or different from this.

He follows, himself, in several months.

Assume a god, or a set of them,
playful or mean, who toy with us.
What is the worst they can do
to our Lorenzo?
                    Put on *Una cosa rara*
in London and have it succeed.
Let them admire da Ponte
now that he's out of the way.
                              Put on Mozart,
La clemenza di Tito first, and *Die Zauberflöte*
(done in Italian), and then, in 1811,
                                    Così fan tutte.
Figaro the following year.
Da Ponte thousands of miles away, has no idea,
might as well be as dead as Mozart.

In 1817, *Don Giovanni* triumphs
in London,

which, for all it matters to him,
                    is China, the moon . . .

That's never the point,
but then what is? Does it make
any difference?
Either way one answers,
the implications are dreadful.

If we suppose he was better than he knew,
that makes him a tool, a toy, and cozens him
of what any man deserves—
                    the fruits of his labor.

That black water he crosses
surges and falls back, in waves,
predictable tides, idiotic, relentless,
as if there were sense,
as if, with sufficient energy, one might
swim to some safe haven, reach dry land.

Not merely a strange place, but the home of strangeness,
the land stretching away west to vertiginous

spaces beyond the imagination.
Philadelphia first,
then New York, where Nancy is living.

The Grahls have done well, chemists, merchants, physicians.
Lorenzo and Nancy cross the river, settle
in Jersey, open a grocery store
                                        in Elizabeth.

He writes how he laughed
"every time my poetical hand weighed out
two ounces of tea, or cut a plug of tobacco
for some cobbler or carter."
Thus amused, he never notices how
people cheat him, take his kindness as weakness
and him for all he is worth—
                                        seven thousand dollars
going, gone.

And Nancy bears him a son,
a last child, christened Charles Grahl
da Ponte
            (Lorenzo will always call him Carlo).
What to do to eat?
                              Teach perhaps?
                                        Italian?

Maybe Latin?
Something will turn up.
There may yet be something good around the corner.
He sells the house
and they return to New York.

There are more corners there.

You wake from a dream you cannot remember,
try this setting or that, make odd suggestions,
but nothing speaks.
That wasn't it. The kernel
of meaning is gone, and you are the empty husk.

What was there?
The color of lilacs?
Their scent?
You let your mind go blank but all you have
is a blank mind,
which is all you deserve.

In a bookstore on Broadway . . .
(If he has any church or synagogue,

if he believes in anything, feels at home
anywhere, it will be in bookstores.)
In a bookstore, then, on Broadway, where he is browsing,
he enters into a casual conversation
with a younger man, a stranger.
An idle remark,
an answer, a joke, perhaps, and then an allusion,
a reference,
a password . . .
It is Clement Moore, the poet, later famous—
he will write "The Night Before Christmas."
They talk of books,
even Italian books and writers. Moore,
in his late twenties, is charmed by the foreign man
in his middle sixties.
His father, Bishop Moore, is President Moore
of Columbia College.
Clement brings da Ponte
home, and they start a class there in Italian
language and literature.
It's a job,
a respectable calling. He is the *caro maestro*
bringing culture, tradition, refinement,
to these eternally young, impossibly eager

innocents.

This is not what he wanted,
nowhere near what he knows he deserves,
but tolerable.

An end, at least, to the torments
he hasn't deserved either.

A remission then?

Stay there, settle, be content,
we tell him, looking back from the future's heaven,
where we know what the gods know.

He won't, can't,
has no idea who he is, what he ought to do,
what he should settle for.

This was the loss
back in Ceneda, that wrenched from him the name
his mother called him.

Why not take the suggestion
the country offers, however absurd? The country
is large, limitless, strange, a great slattern
welcoming any and all. His in-laws have moved
to Sunbury, a Pennsylvania town
but frontier still, on the Susquehanna River.
Why not go there, trade, sell liquor, grain,
spices, medicines?

The woods are rich in game,
the water clear as Como or Garda. They move,
to start a new life in a new place,
to put down roots and end
these vicissitudes, this endless turning-over
of new pages.
The book still reads the same,
a brief prospering, then the slipping-away
of gains, the always innocent lamb
swindlers recognize as a gift
from God or the devil for them to fleece.

A terrible businessman! He folds,
goes to Philadelphia. She sells hats;
he teaches, or tries to,
finds two pupils,
only two,
while a stern landlady drills
for the rent, the rent, the rent.
Nothing is changed.
Soon he is selling his books again,
his clothing . . .
A letter comes
from Moore, in New York, a reprieve, an invitation
to come back, teach there.

He has learned and accepts.
Or is it a temporizing, a compromise,
a tactical, provisional retreat?

It is hard to say what's in his mind, but he stays,
lives in New York for another nineteen years
and dies there.

But all the time, in his heart
is the feeling children have
that none of this is real, or if it is,
then only for now. Something will happen, new
teeth will come in, bones grow, hair will grow,
there will be changes: a real self, a real world
will emerge in which I will be no longer a stranger
even to myself.

It is 1819.
He is seventy years old.
That adolescence children wait for
in snug cocoons of latency has come
and gone.
There are only disimprovements now
in body and spirit, a settling
for what is,

a recognition that this ill-fitting garment
is what the wardrobe holds.

There is nothing to grow into
but a shroud.

We learn to bear even this, settle, accept,
who have never scribbled a clever verse and heard it
set by Mozart . . .
                                        A gift, but a terrible burden.
This is what God would demand, if there were a god;
this is your authentic self, your talent,
your spirit's heritage.

Weep, then, weep, and dream unbearable dreams
of that life you ought to have led, the amazing work
you ought to have done, the gift you betrayed, and still,
with every breath betray, deny, dishonor.

Look to an empty sky, leaden and low,
and wait for some sign, hope for a dispensation
that has come before and could therefore come again.

It will not come to you.
You have had your chance.

But Byron's poem.
Da Ponte's son Joseph has died,
at twenty-one of consumption.
Prostrate, all but maddened by grief,
Nancy goes into a deep depression.
                                                  Lorenzo
is not in much better case.
                                          One of his students,
hoping to cheer him,
                                    distract him,
                                                  offer him solace,
hands him a copy of Byron's recent piece,
in terza rima
                  (in English!).
It is a curiosity
that speaks deeply, curiously, to da Ponte's
grief:
"The Prophecy of Dante."

This poem Byron wrote in Ravenna, where Dante's
tomb is "one of the principal objects of interest . . .

both to the native and to the stranger."
An exile from England,
Byron had been drawn to Dante's plight
in exile from Florence.
The wars of griefs and angers, Dante's and Byron's,
da Ponte knew, how

"sometimes the last pangs of a vile foe
Writhe in a dream before me and o'er-arch
My brow with hopes of triumph—let them go!
Such are the last infirmities of those
Who long have suffered more than mortal woe,
and yet, being mortal still, have no repose . . . "

The feeling Byron had of being cheated
of what he deserved, by rank and talent, he gave
to Dante, but da Ponte could claim for himself
a little of that. At his tomb, too, would

"pilgrims come from climes where they have known
The name of him, who now is but a name,
And wasting homage o'er the sullen stone,
Spread his—by him unheard, unheeded—fame."

He'll do it! He'll do . . . what? Translate the thing
into Italian, into what terza rima
ought to be. He'll claim the piece for himself.

And does, throwing himself into the work,
and writing with tears streaming down to blur
the words on the page,
"to die is nothing; but to wither thus,
to tame / My mind down
from its own infinity, / To live
in narrow ways with little men,
A common sight to every common eye,
A wanderer,
while even wolves can find a den . . . "

Oh, yes, o si, si . . .

He publishes, and at length receives a letter
from Giagomo Ombrosi, the vice-consul
in Florence, who says a copy was given to Byron
in Leghorn, and the poet
(having taken a villa there for his friend
the Countess
Teresa Guiccioli) received the book
"with much satisfaction."

Si.

He becomes, in 1825, Professor
of Italian at Columbia College—no
stipend, but the title is useful. He can,
at the age of seventy-six now, take in pupils,
to Nancy's boardinghouse, and make a dollar—
he'll lose, of course, as an impresario, bringing
an opera company over to New York.

In 1828, he becomes
a citizen—
a gain, and also a loss,
an acknowledgment.

Nancy dies in 1831. Da Ponte lives on
to 1838. Nearly ninety,
he fails, fades away, sends for a priest,
for form's sake at least.
They keep it quiet
that he, too, is a priest.

"I dreamt of roses and laurels," he wrote,
"but from the roses I had only thorns,
and from the laurels bitterness."

Back in Ceneda,
by now merged with the neighboring Serravalle
into Vittorio Veneto, they name
a street
the Via da Ponte.

Author's Note

I have relied for my information about da Ponte on April Fitzlyon's *The Libertine Librettist* (Abelard Schuman, 1957) and Sheila Hodges' *Lorenzo da Ponte* (Universe Books, 1985).